Printed in Canada
First edition July 2023
ISBN: 978-1-57571-910-8
(hardback)

Designed by Lesley Delchamps

100

Southern Ways

TO SAY

I LOVE YOU

COMPILED & WRITTEN BY KELLY KAZEK
ILLUSTRATED BY WALKER MILLER

Hey, there, Sugar Lump! Let's discuss Southern love ... because who doesn't like to hear someone say, "I love you?" Those three little words are some of the most important in the human experience. Yet, here in the South, we sometimes add a little more, shall we say, flavor to our "I love yous."

Sometimes, it's because we want to make sure our intentions are clear. Sometimes, it's because Cupid needs a hand – he tends to get stuck in a rut, what with the bow and arrows and all those accoutrements.

Then, there are Southern endearments, those pet names we use to refer to loved ones. Plain old "dear" won't cut it. Sure, it's perfectly functional, even practical. It could be used in cases when someone hasn't had coffee and is experiencing brain fog, as in "Oh, you're leaving to start college? Have fun, dear."

But for pet names to be true Southern endearments, they need a little pizazz. A little whimsy. Some downright silliness. Like "sweetie," "honey bun," or "sugar."

In an article by Jeremy B. Jones on OurState.com, he surmises Southerners choose such fun and cheeky endearments because: a. we like sweets and b. we're polite and endearments help soften harsh statements ... kind of like "bless your heart."

The more common endearments have been around for years, Jones said. "We've been using sweetness to talk about one another since the 13th century, at least," he said. "'Sweetheart' is more than 700 years old. 'Honey' is more than 600. The Oxford English Dictionary finds evidence of the term 'Cinnamon' as an address in the 14th century." Still, Southerners can take credit for "Sugar" (or at least we're going to), which didn't come on the scene until the 1930s.

For this book, we gathered lots of fun phrases about love and then, just because we can, we made up a few more. What can we say? We're in love with love. ♡

I LOVE YOU MORE THAN

cornbread on Sunday.

I'D GET

gussied up

FOR YOU.

AS LONG AS I'VE GOT A BISCUIT,

you've got half.

I LOVE YOU MORE THAN

biscuits and

gravy.

I LOVE YOU LIKE A

possum

LOVES A

June bug.

WE GO TOGETHER LIKE

country ham

&

red-eye gravy.

I LOVE YOU MORE THAN

pepper sauce

on

collard greens.

I JUST WANT TO

hug your neck.

I LOVE YOU

a bushel.

I'M STUCK ON YOU LIKE

kudzu ON A

junked car.

SURE AS THE VINE TWINES
around the stump,
YOU ARE MY DARLIN'
sugar lump.

YOU'RE MY
Sweet Pea.

WE'RE STUCK TOGETHER LIKE A COUPLE OF

love bugs.

I LOVE YOU MORE THAN
a basket of
peaches in July.

Y'ALL COULD'VE HAD ME AT

hello.

YOU'RE PRETTY AS

a mess of

fried catfish.

LIKE CORNBREAD,
you make
everything better.

I LOVE YOU FROM

can to cain't.

YOU'RE PRETTY AS A

Georgia peach.

YOU REALLY

crank my

tractor.

YOU'RE MY

Sugar Pie.

You've rurnt me

FOR ANYONE ELSE.

I LOVE YOU MORE THAN

my bass boat.

I LOVE YOU MORE THAN

deviled eggs.

I'm besotted!

I COULD JUST

sop you up

with a biscuit.

MY HEART'S FIXIN' TO

bust with love.

YOU'RE MY

Honey Bunch.

YOU'RE YUMMIER THAN

a cat's head biscuit.

I LOVE YOU MORE THAN

Dollar General's
got stores.

YOU'RE PRETTIER THAN
a speckled pup
IN A
little red wagon.

I LOVE YOU MORE THAN

I hate the college football team

YOU ROOT FOR.

I'm carrying
a torch for you.

YOU SING A SONG

only I can hear.

YOU'RE THE

apple of my eye

AND THE

peach of my pie.

I LOVE YOU MORE THAN

Milo's tea!

I LOVE YOU MORE THAN

my pickup truck.

You're the one
I hold dear.

YOU'RE SWEETER THAN

honeysuckle.

YOU'RE NEATER THAN A

Buc-ee's restroom.

YOU'RE SWEETER THAN

a truckload of

Little Debbies.

YOU HAVE A HEART
as big as Texas.

If I had
my druthers,
I'D HAVE YOU.

I'M STUCK ON YOU LIKE

a tick to

a hound.

I LOVE YOU LIKE

a pig loves

sunshine.

YOU MELT MY HEART LIKE

butter on a

biscuit!

YOU'RE LIKE GRAVY:

you make everything better.

I LOVE YOU MORE THAN
college football.

Sure do
'preciate you!

YOU'RE THE
Mason jar to
my preserves.

YOU'RE SWEETER AND

more complicated

THAN LANE CAKE.

YOU'RE YUMMIER THAN
a bag of
boiled peanuts.

YOU'RE SWEETER THAN A

Claxton

Fruit Cake.

YOU'RE MY

Sugar Britches.

YOU'RE MY

Love Muffin.

I LOVE YOU MORE THAN

church lady pie.

YOU'RE SWEETER THAN

Grandma's tea.

UR HOTTER'N A CHILI PEPPER

You're precious
as all get out.

My heart
skips a beat
WHEN YOU COME AROUND.

WE GO TOGETHER LIKE

peanuts and Coke.

I CRAVE YOU MORE THAN

chocolate gravy.

I CAN'T IMAGINE LIFE WITHOUT YOU...
and Goo Goo Clusters.

WE GO TOGETHER LIKE

bananas and

puddin'.

YOU'RE COOLER THAN A BAG OF

Chick-fil-A ice.

YOU MAKE ME

light up like a lightning bug.

I'm smitten with you.

Here are more things to love: fun, Southern-themed books
from It's a Southern Thing!

Check out:
The Southern Thesaurus, all about our colorful phrases and language, and
The Southern Handbook, a handy guide for any Southerner or wanna-be Southerner.
And don't miss our full line of Southern-themed children's books!

store.southernthing.com

Kelly Kazek, an award-winning journalist and humor columnist, writes about the South's culture for It's a Southern Thing. She is the author of *The Southern Thesaurus* and *The Southern Handbook*, ten children's picture books, including *Y is for Y'all*, and several humor collections. She lives near Huntsville, Alabama.

Walker Miller is an illustrator and graphic designer currently living in Irondale, Alabama. While growing up, his mom always made sure he had colored pencils or crayons within reach. When he isn't drawing or designing, he's either skateboarding, reading, or hanging out with his girlfriend and two cats.

It's a Southern Thing serves up relatable humor, inspirational people and fascinating stories that break the stereotypes and show the South as the culturally rich, diverse, down-home place it really is. Visit us at southernthing.com and find us on Facebook, YouTube, Instagram, TikTok and Twitter.